EARTH

EXPLORING THE ELEMENTS: BOOK FOUR

SIMONE AKASHA NOFEL

Dedicated to my niece, Ava.
Stay strong, stay sweet, and keep smiling.

And to you, the reader.
Be kind, be passionate, and keep exploring!

EARTH© Copyright <<November 2021>> Simone Nofel
Place of Publication, Seattle, WA

Book cover design, illustration, editing, and interior layout by:

www.1000storybooks.com

For more information, email support@heartyandfree.com

Hardback ISBN-13: 978-1-957327-11-2

Paperback ISBN-13: 978-1-957327-10-5

eBook ISBN-13: 978-1-957327-09-9

Library of Congress: 2022909633

BEFORE YOU READ:

Go outside and put your bare feet
on the ground.

Sit in your treehouse, if you have
one, or near a window with a view.

Take a deep breath.

I am earth. I am the element that holds humanity and supports all life-forms.

I am not just the name of the planet you live on. I am also all the solid things in nature. Mountains, pinecones, rocks, and flowers are parts of me you might see every day.

I am underneath the ground you walk on as soil and clay. If you look closely, I also hide in the form of deep, dark caves.

I provide shelter and protection to all living things. My treetop canopies and underground burrows are ways I keep some animals safe.

With the plants that grow on me, I give you and other animals nourishment to stay healthy. Eating fruit from my tree branches and vegetables from my soil will keep your body strong.

I am here for your stability, to keep you grounded. Try walking in the grass without shoes or socks to help you feel happy, calm, and relaxed.

Over time, I have been disappearing. Deforestation and some modern agriculture have been hurting me.

When this happens, the homes of animals like deer, squirrels, birds, and insects get destroyed.

All of you can help to keep me vibrant and healthy by learning sustainable ways to live. You can compost food scraps, collect rainwater, recycle, and reuse items for crafts to begin contributing.

You can also grow your own food at home or in a community garden. Planting a variety of fruits and vegetables helps nourish my soil.

FUN FACTS!

- I represent abundance, discipline, nurture, and balance.

- In classical medicines, I am associated with the stomach and spleen.

- I am paired with the color green.

- My common symbols are:

SUGGESTED ACTIVITIES
(ASK YOUR GROWN-UP FOR HELP)

Grow and eat microgreens by learning how to sprout them.

- To find full instructions on the sprouting process for microgreens, visit heartyandfree.com/4kids

Reduce waste and start collecting compost to improve soil health.

- To get help deciding what is appropriate to add to your composting bin, visit heartyandfree.com/4kids

- Don't have a home garden to add your compost to? Visit compostnow.org to see if their doorstep collection services are in your area.

Find more fun at heartyandfree.com/4kids

COMING SOON. . .

Ether

Check heartyandfree.com/4kids for latest releases!

LOVE THIS BOOK?
DON'T FORGET TO LEAVE A REVIEW!

Every review matters, and it matters a lot!

Head over to Amazon or wherever you purchased this book to leave a review for me.

My heart thanks you!

Lightning Source UK Ltd.
Milton Keynes UK
UKHW050304171222
414014UK00004B/51